The Happy Hobgoblin

by Kay Brophy

with illustrations by Katy Boys

First published in the UK in 2016 by Middle Farm Press
British Library Cataloguing-in-Publication Data
A catalogue record for this book is available from the British Library
ISBN 978-0-9928896-5-4

This edition 2020
3 4 5 6 7 8 9 10

Published by Middle Farm Press
Author: Kay Brophy
Managing Editor: Kate Taylor
Illustrator: Katy Boys
Designer: Su Richards
Printed by Think Digital Books Ltd

To my godson, Henry

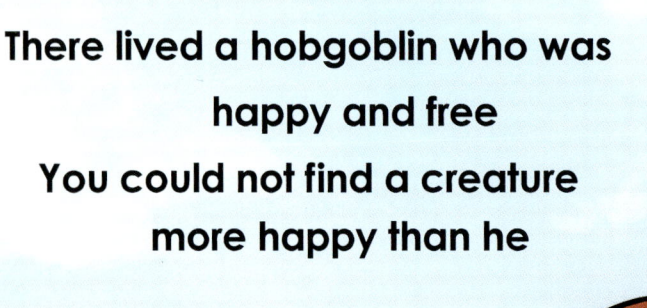

There lived a hobgoblin who was
happy and free
You could not find a creature
more happy than he

Grace · J · Goblin

But let's go back in time when this wasn't the case
When our friend was confused about
family and race
'Who am I?' hobgoblin had started to wonder
'Am I a hob or a goblin, which do I come under?'

HUGH · HOB COARSE FISHING CHAMPION '01

Our hobgoblin was friends with
a brown fox called Ken
He was cunning and clever and lived in a den
So he visited Ken and explained what was wrong
'I need to go on a journey, will you come along?'

Through woods they walked;
over mountains they climbed
Speaking to others, some fierce and some kind
Hobgoblin and Ken travelled far and so wide
Where they learnt about feelings
that lurk deep inside

Then one day there came a loud roar
The hobs and the goblins, it seemed,
were at war!

The hobgoblin tried hard to
listen and understand
'But where do I belong in this
confusing Lostland?'

Then all of a sudden,
he started to sob
'Please help me work out,
am I goblin or hob?'

LIFELAND TIMES

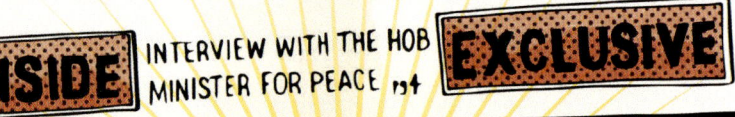

DAILY 50P

TODAYS WEATHER: EXPECT WILD AUTUMNAL WINDS WITH BURSTS OF SUNSHINE 6°C

WAR RAGES ON!

HOBS AND GOBLINS FIGHT FOR A THIRD WEEK

LATEST NEWS:

NEW FEARS AS HOBS AND GOBLINS GO TO WAR.

There has been conflict between the Hobs and Goblins since time began, but this week the hostility reached new heights as fighting took to the streets on a mass scale. It's hard to imagine a peaceful future in Lifeland. Schools have been closed and shops will now only serve 'their own kind'. It's a worrying time and we need to take this war very seriously indeed.

OTHER NEWS

FICTION FROM FAIRIE

★

Our local fairie has started to write under-the-bed story books for kids to help them overcome night-time fears.

FASHION NEWS

skele launches new design label that brings bright and colourful clothes to Lifeland, making even the most miserable person smile

THE BEASTLY BATTLE BEGINS

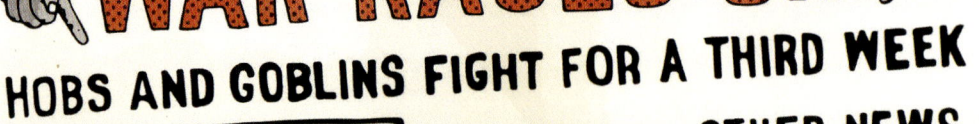

Ken reached out and took his friend by the hand
He knew that this fight was the talk of the land
Ken tilted his head before he began
He would help the hobgoblin,
he would think of a plan

'Well' said Ken 'I understand your pain'
'There is always a lesson to be learned,
some knowledge to gain'

'The problem for the hobs and the goblins is clear'
'They are scared of each other and that
feeling is fear'

'Sometimes when
we're frightened
on the inside'

'We blame others,
fight, or run away
and hide'

'When something is different it can feel quite scary'

'And the feeling is often being worried or wary'

'But you have a choice my hobgoblin friend'
'Which side to take, who to befriend'
'Happiness can be found in the strangest of places'
'In all situations, families, cultures and races'

'I love them both' the hobgoblin
said with a tear
'There is no way I can choose
a favourite here.'

Ken smiled and said 'Then this war
is not yours to fight'
'Their problems aren't yours to fix,
try as you might'

'You are both hob, and goblin,
and proud'
'So face who you are and
say it out loud!'

'I am hob, I am goblin!'
the hobgoblin cried
'And I am proud to belong to
each of these sides!'

The hobgoblin discovered something
important that day
He found out that 'big' feelings CAN go away
And so our hobgoblin now spends his days
Helping others feel happy and
sharing new ways

The Happy Hobgoblin has managed to find happiness in difficult times. Join him as he journeys through 'Lifeland', a magical place where he learns about 'big' feelings. Hobgoblin is helped along the way by his good friend and confidant Ken the fox.

All children, in every walk of life, will struggle with their feelings from time to time. The Finding Your Way series of books focuses on the six 'big' feelings of sadness, fear, anger, happiness, surprise and disgust and aims to show the reader how to explore, identify and manage the feelings safely – on their own or with the help of an adult.

HOW TO USE THIS BOOK
This book can be read with a child or a group of children at any time. It has been specifically written to help educate children about the feeling of *happiness*. Happiness is an emotional response to feeling connected to the world around us and sensory pleasures.

When we feel happiness, it can often change quickly to other feelings, such as surprise, sadness or fear. Children sometimes find it difficult to talk directly to adults about things that confuse them, they tend to show us in their behaviour instead. So rather than focusing on the child, the adult can help by focusing on how the characters are feeling. For example, by asking the child how they think the Hobgoblin is feeling about his family, the child will be encouraged to think about their own experiences of happiness, helping them to explore these feelings in a safe way. Adults can use the pictures within the book to aid them.

USING THE FIVE Ws
Example questions you could ask while reading this book:

- **W**hy does the Hobgoblin need help?
- **W**hat do you think he should do?
- **W**here is he in Lifeland?
- **W**ho helps him to deal with his feelings?
- **W**hen does the Hobgoblin feel happy?

Adults can help the child explore these feelings using the 'Lifeland' map at the front of the book. As you read through the book together, try to encourage the child to think about where Hobgoblin is on the map. For example, when the Hobgoblin is at Ken's house, you could help the child think about where that might be on the map, exploring feelings and places together.

Did you know?
- Reading with your child at least four times a week can help them to develop their own reading and literacy skills.
- Talking to your child about feelings can help them develop their emotional language and intelligence.